CELEBRATIONS AND RITUALS

TOWER HAMLETS COLLEGE
Learning Centre
Arbour Square
LONDON E1 0PT
Tel: 020 7510 7568

marriagecelebrations

CHERRYTREE BOOKS

Published in the UK by Cherrytree Books, part of the
Evans Publishing Group
2A Portman Mansions
Chiltern Street
London W1U 6NR

First published in paperback in 2007.

In the same series:
Celebrating Prophets & Gods
End-of-Life Rituals
Everyday Celebrations and Rituals
Winter Celebrations

British Library Cataloguing-in-Publication Data

Chambers, Catherine
  Marriage. – (Celebrations and rituals)
  1. Marriage customs and rites – Juvenile literature
  I. Title II. Martell, Hazel Mary III. Senker, Cath
  392.5

  ISBN 978 1 84234 401 9

Printed and bound in China by C&C Offset
1 2 3 4 5 6 7 8 9 10 09 08 07 06 05 04 03

McRae Books:
Publishers: Anne McRae and Marco Nardi
Series Editor: Loredana Agosta
Graphic Design: Marco Nardi
Layout: Sebastiano Ranchetti
Picture Research: Loredana Agosta
Cutouts: Filippo delle Monache, Alman Graphic Design
Text: Catherine Chambers, Hazel Mary Martell, Neil Morris,
Cath Senker

Illustrations: Studio Stalio (Alessandro Cantucci, Fabiano
Fabbrucci, Andrea Morandi, Ivan Stalio), MM Illustrazione
(Manuela Cappon), Paola Ravaglia, Paula Holguin, Ferruccio
Cucchiarini

Colour Separations: Litocolor, Florence (Italy)

Copyright © 2003, McRae Books Srl

Borgo La Croce, 8—Florence, Italy.
info@mcraebooks.com

Acknowledgements:
The Publishers would like to thank the following photographers
and picture libraries for the photos used in this book.
t=top; tl=top left; tc=top centre; tr=top right; c=centre;
cl=centre left; cr=centre right; b= bottom; bl=bottom left;
bc=bottom centre; br=bottom right
A.S.A.P Picture Library: 24br, 25cr, 25bl, 28tr, 28br; Dinodia: 18br,
21cr; Lonely Planet Images: Martin Moos 14b, Karen Trist 16b,
Richard I'Anson 17cr, Martin Hughes 17bl, Charlotte Hindle 31tr,
Richard Nebesky 33tr, Christian Aslund 37tl, Mitch Reardon 41cr;
Marco Lanza: 21bl, 31cr; The Image Works: cover, 12cr, 12b, 13tr,
15tr, 15br, 21tr, 22l, 23tl, 26bl, 27cr, 27bl, 31bl, 32cr, 34cl, 35tr,
35bl, 36br, 37cr, 39tr, 39br, 40bl, 42b, 43tl, 43cr

marriagecelebrations

CHERRYTREE BOOKS

Table of Contents

Marriage Celebrations

Introduction

The union of two people in marriage is a part of all human societies in some form or another. Through history, the importance of marriage as a bond between two people has been expressed through the various rituals and customs that have developed over time and survived with passing generations. In many cultures, weddings unite families or clans, as well as two individuals. In some societies, marriages are often arranged by family members or matchmakers, who carefully select suitable partners or introduce men and women to one another. In other societies, where individuals choose their own partners, couples usually spend a period of time dating or getting to know each other before committing to marriage. Regardless of how couples are brought together, weddings are joyous occasions. For many, the period before the wedding is a special time of preparation and planning, enriched by rituals and ceremonies. In Hindu culture, for example, a couple pledges to marry at a formal engagement ceremony during which they pray for blessings. Marriage ceremonies symbolise the union of a couple through various rituals. These include exchanging rings or gifts, joining hands or tying garments together. After the ceremony is completed, lavish feasts and dancing often celebrate the couple and their new life together.

Renaissance waiters bring out food at a wedding banquet. During the Renaissance (from the early 1300s to about 1600), wedding feasts were extravagant occasions. They were opportunities for royalty and nobles to show off their power and wealth.

In many cultures, gifts, known as the bride price, are given to the bride or her family by the prospective husband. Necklaces of amber and silver are often part of the bride price in Somalia in northeastern Africa.

The ancient Roman marriage ceremony was non-religious. Once the bride and groom gave their consent to the marriage, they joined right hands. This Roman marble relief shows the bride and groom and the pronuba (matron of honour) behind them. The pronuba was a married woman who assisted during the wedding ceremony.

WEDDING SYMBOLS AND THEIR MEANINGS

CHINA
Lotus seeds—fertility

FIJI
Whale's tooth, called tabua—bride's status

GREECE
Crowns—the couple as king and queen of their household

INDIA
Henna tattoos on the bride—strong love

ITALY
Sugared almonds, called confetti—sweet and bitter things in life

JAPAN
Crane, bird—a long and faithful marriage

JEWISH
Huppah—the shelter of God's love, the couple's home

NORTHERN AFRICA
Calabashes—bride's wealth

SPAIN
Thirteen coins, called arras—groom's pledge to care for bride

Marriage Through History

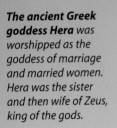

The ancient Greek goddess Hera was worshipped as the goddess of marriage and married women. Hera was the sister and then wife of Zeus, king of the gods.

A married couple in an Egyptian statue are the same height. This shows that they were equally important.

Although wedding ceremonies have varied among cultures and over time, most have included a feast for the families of the bride and groom and invited guests. This is still often the case today.

Tying the Knot in Ancient Mexico

Aztec men married at about age 20. A man's parents looked for a wife a few years younger than their son. Then they asked a soothsayer (a person who attempts to tell the future) if the couple was suited to each other according to the stars. If all was well, one or more older women from the groom's family went to the girl's parents to ask for her hand in marriage. If the girl's parents agreed, preparations began for a great feast. On the wedding day, the bride dressed with great ceremony. She was carried to the groom's house, where the young couple sat on a mat in front of the hearth.

Ancient Egyptian Contract

In ancient Egypt, young men usually married from about age 15 to 20. Their brides were usually two or three years younger. Sometimes a marriage contract was drawn up. It listed what the husband and wife would own separately after they wed and what they would own jointly. It also set out how the property would be distributed in case of death or divorce. There was no wedding ceremony. The newly married couple simply brought all their possessions to their new home.

An Aztec groom's cloak was tied to his bride's dress. The knot showed that they were married. A huge feast followed the wedding.

Wedding Processions in Ancient Greece

A wedding ceremony in ancient Greece consisted of a series of rituals. One of the most important events was the wedding procession, which took the bride from her father's house to her new husband's home. Before leaving, the bride took a special bath and sat veiled while a great feast took place. Unveiling the bride in front of the groom was an important part of the ritual. At last, her family saw her off, and she was carried to her husband's home and a new life as a married woman.

Sometimes, Greek townspeople joined in a wedding procession. When a bride arrived at her new home, she was showered with flowers, fruit and nuts.

Ancient Rome

Women in ancient Rome had no legal rights except through their father or husband. The paterfamilias (head) of a Roman household had complete power over all its members. Parents chose marriage partners for their children, usually without considering the children's opinions or preferences. Many marriages were arranged for economic or political benefit. In well-to-do families, boys usually married when they were 15 to 18 years old, and girls when they were 13 or 14. Marriage celebrations of wealthy Romans could be extravagant events. The ceremony usually took place in the bride's home and included a sacrifice to the gods and an elaborate feast. The bride was taken in procession to the bridegroom's home, where she was lifted across the threshold. The origin of this custom is unknown. It may have been done out of respect for the Roman goddess Cardea, who was associated with door frames and hinges and symbolically, family life.

This portrait of a husband and wife comes from the Roman town of Pompeii.

Christ blesses a Christian bridal couple in an image found in a Roman catacomb. Catacombs are systems of underground passages and rooms used as ancient burial places. Paintings on the walls and ceilings of Roman catacombs represent some of the earliest examples of Christian art.

A medieval friar joins the hands of a bride and groom.

Marriage in the Middle Ages

Marriage in a Christian church gradually replaced non-religious marriage ceremonies for many Europeans during the Middle Ages (a period from about the A.D. 400s to the 1400s). But some Roman wedding customs became part of the sacred Christian celebration of holy matrimony. These include the bridal veil and the gift of a wedding ring.

The Dowry

In Italy, during a period called the Renaissance (the early 1300s to about 1600) fathers were expected to provide their daughters with a dowry. A dowry was a gift of money or property brought by a bride to her husband when they married. Women with a large dowry attracted more suitors. As a result, many men began saving for a dowry at their daughter's birth. In Florence and other Italian cities, beautiful wooden chests were often bought with dowry money.

A painted dowry chest, made in Florence in about 1472, held a bride's linen, clothing and jewellery.

PEOPLE BEGAN WEARING A WEDDING RING on the third finger of the left hand in ancient times. They believed that a vein or nerve ran directly from that finger to the heart. According to some traditions, a wedding ring should have no gems so that it, like the couple's love, will have no end. Diamond engagement rings became popular in the late 1800s and 1900s. Diamonds, the hardest natural substance, represent eternal love.

Chinese Traditions

A Chinese marriage is considered a union between two families as well as two individuals. Traditionally, the bride left her family to become part of her husband's family. The marriage process began with a proposal made by the couple's parents. Next, an astrologer (a person who tells fortunes by studying the stars) determined whether the pair would be a good match. At the engagement ceremony, the groom's parents presented gifts to the bride's parents, and an auspicious (lucky) wedding date was chosen. Then the bride's family presented her dowry. The betrothal could last for a year or two—or, for children, until the girl and boy had grown up. In modern China, many young people choose their own partners, though they may still follow treasured customs.

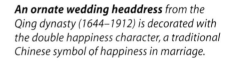

Preparing for the Big Day in Times Past

On the day before the wedding, a good-luck man or woman—someone who had been lucky in life—moved the bridal bed to a favourable location and placed good-luck fruits and nuts on it. Children, a symbol of fertility, were invited to scramble around the bed for the food. The night before the wedding, the bride had her hair combed and the groom had a special cap placed on his head. These rituals signalled that they were now adults.

The seeds of the lotus flower along with red dates, oranges, peanuts and pomegranates, were placed on the bridal bed.

An ornate wedding headdress from the Qing dynasty (1644–1912) is decorated with the double happiness character, a traditional Chinese symbol of happiness in marriage.

A bride is carried to her new husband's home in a sedan chair. The sedan chair was closed to protect her from evil spirits and to prevent her from seeing anything considered unlucky.

The Bride's Journey

On the day of the wedding, the groom sent a sedan chair (a covered chair for one person carried on poles by two or more men) to the bride's home. The chair was decorated in red, the colour of happiness. Musicians accompanied the groom and his attendants, playing wedding music all the way. At the bride's house, the groom's party was met by the bride's friends. They refused to give up the young woman until they were satisfied with the gifts the groom had brought. Much good-natured bargaining took place. Eventually, the bride got into the sedan chair and, accompanied by the musicians and her attendants, left for her husband's home.

The Chinese Double Happiness character is printed on red paper and placed where a young couple will see it at their wedding. It represents the wish that the two will experience happiness together.

The Far East

THE FAR EAST

The Far East is the easternmost part of Asia. Asia extends from Africa and Europe in the west to the Pacific Ocean in the east. The northernmost part of the continent is in the Arctic. In the south, Asia ends in the tropics near the equator. Traditionally, the term Far East has referred to China, Japan, North Korea, South Korea, Taiwan and eastern Siberia in Russia. Southeast Asia includes Borneo, Brunei, Cambodia, East Timor, Indonesia, Laos, Malaysia, Myanmar, the Philippines, Singapore, Thailand and Vietnam.

Modern Chinese Weddings

Nowadays, the bride's family usually does not offer a dowry. Wedding guests bring red envelopes filled with money or jewellery for the couple, to help them start their new life together. During the wedding ceremony and banquet, the bride changes clothes several times. It is a traditional custom thought to provide the opportunity for the bride to show off her wealth. Today, the custom allows the bride to wear both Chinese and Western costumes at the event. At Buddhist weddings in China, the couple chooses the scriptures they read. They exchange vows, and their families bless the marriage.

The tea served to the groom's parents at the wedding ceremony traditionally has two lotus seeds or two red dates in each cup as a symbol of fertility.

Wedding Ceremony

A traditional Chinese wedding was simple. The bride and groom went to the family altar to pray to the gods and to the family ancestors. Then the bride served tea to the groom's parents. The bride and groom completed the ceremony by bowing to each other. In some regions, they both drank wine from the same goblet and ate a lump of sugar shaped like a rooster. Roosters were believed to ward off evil and bad luck.

A Chinese couple pose with friends and relatives dressed in Western-style clothes after a Buddhist wedding ceremony in Taiwan.

THE SEVENTH LUNAR MONTH (around late August on the Western calendar) is inauspicious (unlucky) for weddings. It is the time of the Hungry Ghost Festival, when lost spirits from hell wander on Earth— and might turn up at a wedding!

After the Wedding

Traditionally, the groom's family gave a lavish wedding banquet in their home. Now, the banquet is usually held in a restaurant. It gives the bride's and groom's parents the opportunity to publicly announce their children's marriage. A traditional Chinese banquet has about 12 courses, including roast pig, shark fin soup, rice, noodles and dessert. In some places, the couple follows the custom of visiting the bride's family three days after the wedding.

An altar dedicated to the family's ancestors plays an important part in traditional weddings.

NU WA, DIVINE MATCHMAKER

According to Chinese mythology, the goddess Nu Wa invented marriage. One legend tells how after Earth was created, Nu Wa lived there alone. But she was lonely. One day, she decided to make living creatures that looked like her. She mixed mud with water and created little clay figures that she brought to life. Nu Wa divided the people into men and women. After some of them grew old and died, she taught people how to reproduce and raise children.

Traditional Japanese Weddings

In Japan, many couples have their wedding ceremony at a Shinto shrine (a place sacred to a religion). Shinto is the ancient traditional religion of Japan. The bride dresses in a kimono, and a Shinto priest conducts the ceremony. Only close family members and friends attend the ceremony. Very few Japanese still follow the custom of arranged marriages. Such couples are introduced by a go-between. If they like each other, they meet again and get to know each other better. They may meet several people before they find someone they really like. If a couple gets along well, they usually marry, though the final decision is up to them. Nowadays, most couples meet and marry in the Western style, out of love. Weddings often feature a mixture of Japanese and Western customs.

The crane is a popular Japanese symbol of long life. It often appears on the bride's kimono and as a table decoration at the wedding reception to wish the couple a long and faithful marriage.

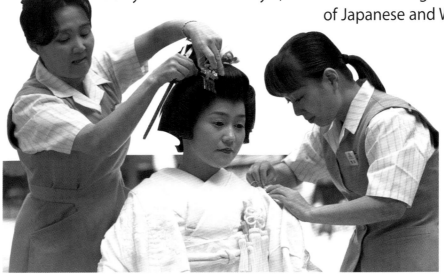

A bride is prepared for wedding photos at Meiji-jingu Shrine, a beautiful Shinto shrine in Tokyo.

The Traditional Bride

Once the couple have decided to marry, they become betrothed. This stage is called yui-no, which means to apply. The two families meet for dinner and exchange a series of about ten symbolic gifts. At Shinto weddings, the bride wears a wig decorated with artificial flowers, gold combs and maybe even pearls. Her kimono is pure white.

The Go-Between

Before a man and woman are introduced, their parents make up a packet of information about them. It tells all about their son's or daughter's education, achievements and interests and includes a photograph. The information goes to a go-between, a man who matches couples that seem suited to each other. The go-between arranges a meeting. He comes along—and so do the parents—to make sure everything progresses smoothly!

One traditional wedding custom is for the bride and groom to ride in a gondola (a long, narrow boat). Behind the bride is her go-between, who is always a man, and his wife.

AT A JAPANESE WEDDING, THE GROOM MAY CRACK A RAW EGG with his bare foot. The egg may be a symbol of fertility and the hope that the couple will have many children. It also may be a symbol of how fragile life and love are. Another tradition calls for ducks or two geese to accompany the groom. Because ducks and geese mate for life, they are a symbol of faithfulness.

A Shinto Wedding

A traditional Japanese wedding takes place at a Shinto shrine. Wedding palaces, where weddings usually take place now, also have shrines. At the ceremony, the kami, (spirits that live all over Earth) are honoured. The bride and groom face the Shinto shrine. After saying a prayer, the priest makes a food offering to the kami. He waves a stick with white streamers called the harai-gushi to purify everyone there. Then the bride and groom share sake, a wine made from rice, and say their vows. They may then exchange rings. Often a couple will have a Western-style ceremony as well. A reception follows the ceremony. Many women change into a Western-style white dress for this occasion.

At a wedding at a Shinto shrine, a couple walks under a red lacquered umbrella, a symbol of good luck.

A priest hands a bride a cup of sake during a wedding ceremony.

Sake

Sharing sake is the heart of the wedding ceremony. The groom takes three sips from the first of three cups. The bride follows him, and then they follow the same procedure with the second and third cups. More sake is then served to close family members.

Three cups are used for serving sake at a wedding ceremony. Sake is a type of Japanese wine made from rice.

The husband and wife rocks are tied together with a rope made of rice straw.

THE HUSBAND AND WIFE ROCKS

The husband and wife rocks, called the Meotoiwa, are a pair of rocks near Futamigaura Beach, which lies along the southern coast of central Honshu, near the city of Ise. According to Shinto legend, these rocks sheltered Izanagi and Izanami, the male and female kami who created the Japanese islands. The two rocks are joined by a sacred rope made from rice straw. Such ropes are used to mark all sacred trees, rocks or shrines, which are considered dwelling places of the gods. The rope is replaced at a festival every 5 January. The torii (gate) on top of the larger rock is another Shinto symbol that marks off shrines and other sacred places. Shinto tradition says that newlyweds who witness the spectacular sunset between the rocks will have a happy marriage.

Weddings in Korea and Southeast Asia

Because there are many religions in Korea and Southeast Asia, marriage customs vary across the region. Most South Koreans are Buddhists or Confucians, while the Communist government of North Korea discourages all religion. Islam is the major religion in Indonesia and Malaysia. Buddhism is important in Thailand and Christianity in the Philippines. In these countries, however, family ties are generally strong, and weddings are considered important social events. People still practise traditional ceremonies and rituals in many parts of the region. Couples often keep traditional practices alive by including them in modern ceremonies.

A gold earring from the island of Sumba is typical of the beautiful jewellery traditionally worn at Indonesian weddings.

Wild Geese

In South Korea, a bridegroom traditionally visits his bride's family home before the wedding ceremony to present his future mother-in-law with a wild goose. The goose is a symbol of faithfulness because geese mate for life. The goose also represents order and harmony, because geese fly in orderly groups. When the groom reaches his bride's house, he places the goose on a small table that serves as the ceremonial altar.

Wooden wild geese represent a new husband and wife. Wooden models have taken the place of live geese in modern Korea.

AT TRADITIONAL KOREAN WEDDINGS A HEN AND ROOSTER ARE PUT UNDER THE WEDDING TABLE. The crowing rooster represents the beginning of a bright new day. The hen is a symbol of hope that the bride will have many children. After the ceremony, the groom's mother throws dates and chestnuts at the bride. The number the bride catches supposedly predicts the number of children the couple will have.

A South Korean bride and groom follow their young attendants. Brides traditionally wore colourful robes, but now they usually follow Western style and wear white.

Korean Tradition

South Koreans believe marriage is more than the joining of two people—it represents the union of two families. Matchmakers are usually employed to find exactly the right husband or wife, and the two sets of parents meet each other first. A fortune-teller then advises on the best date for the wedding. The traditional wedding ceremony is still widely practised today. It takes place at the house of the bride's family. The groom and his attendants walk or ride there in a solemn procession. After the groom reaches the house, attendants lead him and the bride to the area set aside for the ceremony. There, special items, such as a hen and a rooster— symbols of the bride and groom—and a bamboo stick—a symbol of virtue and faithfulness—are placed on the wedding table.

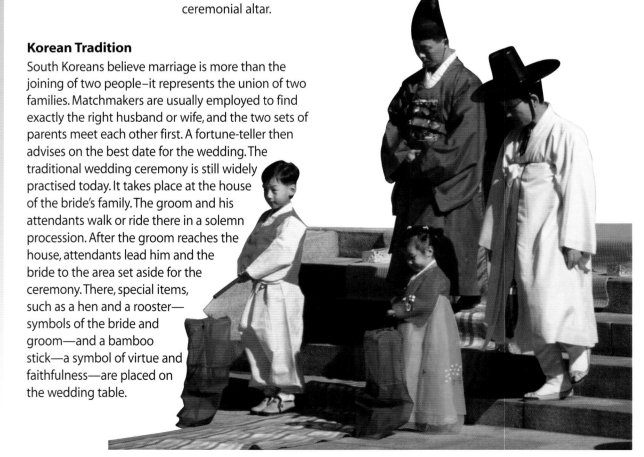

Bridal King and Queen

In Malaysia, the bride and groom are traditionally treated like royalty. At the wedding, they "sit in state", like a king and queen. Sometimes they change costumes several times during the day, putting on special clothes for the official wedding photographs. In previous times, the bride's father and the groom secretly agreed to a contract listing what the groom would pay for his bride and what her dowry would include. Today, the bride is always asked if she consents to the marriage, but the father and groom still negotiate on the bride price and dowry.

A Malay bride and groom sit in state on a decorated platform at their wedding.

A Lisu "courting bag" is worn by marriageable young men. It is made of cloth and covered with tiny coloured beads.

Lisu Bride Price

The Lisu live in scattered mountain villages in Thailand, where they grow rice. Young people are expected to follow strict courtship rituals. When a couple wishes to marry, the young man sends a go-between to the young woman's father. They discuss the amount of valuable black cloth—used to make men's jackets and women's tunics—that will be given to the future bride's family. Many meetings take place to discuss money until a final bride price is agreed upon. Then the two families have a ceremony to bless the marriage.

A Balinese bride appears in her beautiful wedding gown.

A Batak man's bracelet is worn on the right arm. Gold or silver jewellery is often given as a wedding gift and becomes a family heirloom.

Batak Wedding Gifts

Like many other ethnic groups in Indonesia, the Batak people of Sumatra live in clans (large groups of families). A young man is expected to choose a wife from another clan, preferably the one from which his mother came. Gifts are exchanged between the clans. The groom's family usually gives spears, livestock or precious jewellery. The bride's family often offers textiles or food, such as cooked rice, fish and, especially, pork.

Balinese Customs

Most people on the Indonesian island of Bali follow a local version of Hinduism. The marriage of a Hindu couple is an important event in Balinese social life. The wedding usually takes place in the groom's house and is performed by a priest. Either before the wedding or on the wedding day, the bride and groom have their teeth filed, if they haven't already had them filed as children. The middle six upper teeth are ground down to make them even. This custom is considered both a beauty treatment and a way of controlling such human passions as anger and greed.

A silver toe-ring, like the one above, from the state of Orissa in eastern India, is given to a young bride on her wedding day. The fish, a symbol of fertility, is jointed so it seems to swim as the bride walks.

Preparations for a Hindu Wedding

In India, vivahas (weddings) are usually Hindu or Muslim ceremonies. Because of their importance, marriages are often arranged by a couple's parents. Preparations and ceremonies go on for several days before the wedding itself, which is always a colourful affair with everyone wearing brightly coloured clothes and jewellery. The night before a Hindu wedding, the bride and groom each celebrates a Ghari puja with his or her own family. They ask for blessings from the gods by offering grains, coconut and spices.

Pre-wedding Rituals

Before the wedding, both families attend a formal engagement ceremony, called a misri. It starts with seven married women making the symbol for Ganesa, the god of wisdom, on a pot of crystallised sugar and asking for his blessings on the couple. The couple and their parents pray to the gods and ask for their blessings. Then the future bride and groom give each other garlands as a symbol of welcome and gold rings as symbols of a long and happy marriage. Next, the groom's family gives the bride-to-be gifts to show that they accept her. Finally, the groom's family formally agrees to the marriage and feeds the bride's family the sugar to confirm the engagement.

The bride and groom exchange garlands, which can be made from a variety of materials, including flowers, fruits, ribbon and beads.

Mehndi (henna powder) symbolises the strength of love in a marriage, with a darker colour representing a stronger love.

South and Central Asia

SOUTH AND CENTRAL ASIA

South and Central Asia are areas of distinct cultures and peoples. These regions form an area at the base of Asia. Asia extends from Africa and Europe in the west to the Pacific Ocean in the east. The northernmost part of the continent is in the Arctic. In the south, Asia ends in the tropics near the equator. South Asia is made up of Afghanistan, Armenia, Bangladesh, Bhutan, India, the Maldives, Nepal, Pakistan, Sri Lanka, the Tibetan plateau in southwest China and parts of the countries of Azerbaijan and Georgia. Much of India, the largest country in south Asia, forms a peninsula that extends southward into the Indian Ocean. Central Asia includes the countries of Kazakhstan, Kyrgyzstan, Tajikistan, Turkmenistan, Uzbekistan and the West Siberian Plain.

Mehndi

The ritual of Mehndi is celebrated by Hindu brides on the day before their wedding. In the late afternoon, her female relatives and friends gather at the home of the bride's parents. They make a paste from mehndi (henna powder), oil, lemon juice and water tinted with tea, which they use to paint intricate designs on the bride's hands and feet. This takes from about two to several hours, after which everyone has dinner. The next day, the paste flakes off, leaving the designs temporarily stained on the skin.

Sukra is the god of the planet Venus and influences love, passion, beauty and wealth.

Navagraha Puja

For centuries, Indian astrologers have believed that the heavenly bodies influence people and their destinies. The sun, the moon and the major planets are considered the most powerful, and each has its own god who influences different areas of life. Together these gods are known as the Navagrahas. A ceremony called the Navagraha puja is held after the misri ceremony but a few days before the wedding. All the gods are asked to bless the couple and their families. The Navagrahas and their English equivalents are Surya (Sun), Chandra (Moon), Mangala (Mars), Buddha (Mercury), Guru (Jupiter), Sukra (Venus) and Sani (Saturn). Two other gods, Rahu and Ketu, are unique to Hindu tradition.

EACH REGION OF INDIA has its own traditions for bridal clothing. For example, southern brides wear a yellow silk sari with a wide, gold belt and flowers in their hair. In the west, they wear green and decorate their hair with pearls. Northern brides wear red, while in the northeast they wear red and white.

The Bride

Each bride is ritually cleansed in a mixture of tumeric and oils before she puts on her wedding clothes, jewellery and makeup. The details of her outfit depend on the traditions in the area where she lives. But all brides wear a beautiful silk sari with a silk scarf over part of their hair or a veil over their face. The silk is embroidered with gold and silver thread and is often decorated with jewels or pearls. Many brides wear flowers or jewels in their hair. They also wear earrings, necklaces and bracelets of gold, silver or ivory. Their makeup also varies according to local customs.

A bride's earrings from Tamil Nadu in southeast India consist of a round kammal, worn on the earlobe; the jimikki hanging from it; and the maattal, which hooks on to the hair above the ears to support the earring's weight.

A groom in Kerala rides to his wedding on horseback. The music of the accompanying band announces his arrival.

The Groom

On his wedding day, a groom makes his way on horseback to the wedding in a procession of his family and close friends, accompanied by musicians. The groom wears a white satin shirt and dhoti (loose pants). At the wedding location, the groom is received by the bride's mother, who places a tika (dot) of kumkum (red powder) on his forehead for luck, then escorts him to the ceremony.

A bride's father applies a tika to her forehead. This sign, made from sandalwood paste, is a symbol of the third eye of the powerful Hindu god Shiva.

Hindu Weddings

In Hinduism, marriage marks the start of gruhastha (family), one of the four stages of life, according to the Vedas (Hindu sacred books). It is one of the most important samskaras (sacraments) in the Hindu religion and is thought to unite the bride and groom spiritually as well as physically. Hindus believe that a man is not complete until he is married and sure of his wife's support. Both these ideas are represented in many of the rituals that take place on the wedding day. The groom is viewed as Vishnu, the supreme god, and the bride is viewed as Lakshmi, the supreme goddess.

A silver kalasam (pot) is decorated to represent Varalakshmi, worshipped by married women as the protector of wealth.

This wood carving from the early 1800s shows a couple joining hands.

The Symbolism of Fire

After the joining of hands, the priest lights a ceremonial fire to represent the god Vishnu, and the bride and groom make their vows in front of it. The bride's brothers are then called forward to lead her and her husband around the fire three or four times. The number varies according to local custom. As they walk, they throw rice, ghee (clarified butter) and flowers, into the fire to invite the gods to bless the couple with wealth, health, prosperity and happiness. Then the bride and groom take seven steps together while chanting seven oaths, which symbolise seven blessings for their future journey together. The rest of the relatives are then invited into the mandap to congratulate the newly married couple and wish them a long, happy life together.

AT A HINDU WEDDING, the coconut, below, is a symbol of fertility, while rice nourishes life and fire banishes darkness. Fresh flowers symbolise beauty, while kumkum (a red powder) brings good fortune.

The Joining of Hands

Once the groom has arrived at the wedding location, he enters the mandap (wedding canopy). A partition is held in front of the groom and not removed until he says he accepts the bride. The bride is then brought into the mandap by one of her uncles. A purification ritual follows, in which the bride's parents wash the couple's feet with milk and water and put a garland of raw cotton and coloured threads on each of them. Because they are giving their daughter to the groom's family, they then put her right hand in his right hand in a ritual known as hasta-melap, and fasten the hands with a thread that has been blessed. The corner of the bride's sari is also tied to a scarf worn by the groom as a symbol of the bond that will bind them forever.

An agni (ritual fire) burns in a copper container. *The agni, thought to be the mouth of Vishnu, is a symbol of knowledge and happiness.*

Arranged Marriages

Many Hindu marriages are arranged by parents. This is especially true in Indian villages where about 75 percent of the Indian population lives and the tradition of the caste system remains strong. Caste is a social class to which a person belongs at birth. Although the Indian constitution forbids discrimination based on caste, parents still often look for a bride or groom from the same caste. They also search for a person well-suited to their son or daughter and hope that love will grow between them. In the past, marriages were arranged by parents when their children were very young. But now children are included in marriage discussions, and they must be at least 14 years old.

The wedding is held in a mandap, a wooden canopy held up by four decorated pillars representing the four parents involved in the ceremony.

A thaali is a special necklace worn by married women in southern India. The symbols on the thaali show details of a woman's status and her family history.

After the Ceremony

The wedding ceremony is followed by a reception for the bride and groom and their guests. Afterwards, they go to the groom's family home. There, the bride covers her head and sprinkles milk in every corner of the house as a symbol of her respect for her new family. She then picks up a handful of salt and gives it to her husband. He hands it back to her and they repeat the process twice. The bride repeats the ritual with each member of her husband's family. This ceremony is known as Datar and signifies that, just as salt blends in and adds to a dish, so the new bride will blend in with her new family and add to it.

GANESA, ONE OF THE MOST POPULAR HINDU GODS, is the son of Shiva and his consort, Parvati. He is always shown with an elephant's head because when he was young, according to one legend, Shiva chopped his head off with an axe and replaced it with the head of the first animal he saw. All Hindu ceremonies ask for Ganesa's blessing first, to ensure that the ceremony will go well.

A Hindu bride receives a blessing from her new husband's parents on arriving at their home.

Sikh and Parsi Weddings

India has about 14 million Sikhs, who live mainly in the northern state of Punjab, and about 75,000 Parsi, who live mainly in the city of Mumbai. Both religions have wedding ceremonies that are deeply religious, even though they do not necessarily take place in a temple. Sikhs and Parsis celebrate weddings in a joyful way, with many old customs to ensure happiness and prosperity for the couple. Weddings are very colourful, with both brides and grooms wearing garlands around their neck. Sikh and Parsi brides also wear a great deal of jewellery, and their wedding clothes are often embroidered with gold or silver thread.

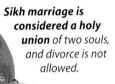

THE *GURU GRANTH SAHIB* consists of poems and hymns composed by six of Sikhism's gurus and other holy men, as well as verses attributed to Guru Nanak, the founder of the Sikh religion. The book is treated with respect and placed on a throne in the gurdwara (temple), because Guru Gobind Singh, the tenth and last guru, who died in 1708, told the Sikhs that the next guru would be the sacred scripture rather than a living person.

The language of the Guru Granth Sahib *is a mixture of Punjabi and Hindi,* written in Gurmukhi script, the sacred writing of the Sikhs.

Sikh Weddings

A Sikh wedding can be held anywhere the *Guru Granth Sahib*, the Sikhs' sacred book, is installed. The ceremony can be conducted by a priest or by any male or female Sikh. The bride's father joins the bride and groom by placing one end of a scarf in the groom's hand and the other end in the bride's hand. The four verses of a prayer called the Lavan hymn are read, and at the end of each verse, the bride and groom walk around the *Guru Granth Sahib*, making their vows.

Sikh marriage is considered a holy union of two souls, and divorce is not allowed.

Guru Ram Das is also remembered for founding Amritsar, *the Sikhs' most sacred city. The Golden Temple, which houses the original copy of the* Guru Granth Sahib, *lies in Amritsar.*

The Lavan Hymn

The fourth guru (teacher) of the Sikh religion was Guru Ram Das (1534–1581). His hymn, Lavan, is the centre of the Sikh marriage ceremony. He wrote it originally to celebrate the union between the human soul and God, which he considered the model for married life. Lavan is a Sanskrit word meaning to break away. It represents the bride breaking away from her parents' home when she marries.

Parsi Pre-wedding Rituals

Parsi weddings last for four days, with the actual ceremony taking place on the evening of the last day. On the first day, a male relative of the groom plants a mango sapling. This is done to wish the couple prosperity and healthy children. On the second day, the couple's formal engagement takes place in the presence of both families. More feasts and festivities follow on the third day, including ceremonies to honour the dead so that the couple will receive blessings from their ancestors. On the wedding day itself, both the bride and the groom are ritually cleansed by the priest. To ward off evil spirits, the bride's mother drops certain foods, such as a raw egg and a coconut, at the feet of the bride and groom.

Three times during the ceremony, the priest asks the couple if they really want to marry. If either the bride or groom answers no, the ceremony ends.

The mango tree is a symbol of fertility.

The Parsi Ceremony

At first, the bride and groom sit facing each other, separated by a curtain but holding hands. The priest passes a cloth rope seven times around their hands, then another rope seven times around their bodies. This symbolises the binding nature of marriage. The curtain is then removed, and the couple sit side by side. They throw rice over each other, then exchange rings while the priest blesses them. Following the ceremony, the couple's friends and relatives enjoy a big party with plenty of food.

A Parsi bride's jewellery is usually a gift from the groom's parents.

LAGAN NU CUSTARD

- 1 litre whole milk
- 200 g sugar
- 180 ml cream
- 8 beaten eggs
- 4 tablespoons ground almonds
- 1 teaspoon crushed cardamom
- ½ teaspoon ground nutmeg
- 2-4 drops vanilla essence
- 1-2 tablespoons rose water
- 1 pinch of salt

Lagan Nu is a traditional Parsi wedding dessert. Heat oven to 150°C/300 °F/gas 2. Meanwhile, pour the milk into a heavy saucepan and bring it to the boil. Reduce heat and simmer until it is reduced by about half. Add sugar and continue to simmer for five minutes, stirring continuously. Remove saucepan from heat, add the remaining ingredients and stir well. Pour mixture into a baking dish. Place dish in a roasting tray of hot water and bake in the oven for one hour. Serve chilled or at room temperature. Cut into pieces to serve.

Muslim Weddings in Central and Southern Asia

Central Asia is made up of several different, independent countries, including Uzbekistan and Tajikistan (which were both part of the former Soviet Union until 1991), Pakistan and Afghanistan. They all have areas of high mountains and deserts, as well as fertile valleys and plains, and the climate can be harsh. Traditionally the people lived by farming or herding animals, and different areas developed their own ways of celebrating. Although Islam has been the dominant religion for many centuries and many people now live in towns and cities, some of the traditional customs are still used, especially at weddings.

Dancing and singing ancient songs to the beat of a drum take place on the second day of wedding celebrations in Pakistan.

A bride and groom in Pakistan are surrounded by family members on their wedding day.

Four Days of Celebration in Pakistan

A Pakistani wedding can include many rituals and celebrations. The first day of festivities, called Mienu, occurs after an engagement is announced. Mienu celebrations are held separately by the families of the bride and groom. A few days before the wedding, the bride's female friends and family gather for a Mehndi party, at which henna is used to create decorative designs on the bride's hands and feet. Shadi is the wedding day itself when the Nikah ceremony (the signing of the marriage contract) takes place. Valima is the groom's family's turn to serve dinner to the wedding guests, who are welcomed by the newly married couple.

Weddings in Uzbekistan

Early autumn is the traditional time for weddings in Uzbekistan. The betrothal is confirmed when the bridegroom's father visits the bride's father and pays him the bride price. This event is celebrated with a banquet for the two families, while the wedding itself (which always takes place on a Friday) is celebrated by the whole community wearing their most colourful outfits. The couple then move to a new house which has been built especially for them.

The wedding ceremony takes place in the mosque where the couple promise to be loyal to each other and to strengthen the alliance between their families.

ISLAM IN CENTRAL ASIA

The Uzbek people live in Uzbekistan, Afghanistan, Tajikistan, Kyrgyzstan and in Kazakhstan, Turkmenistan and Sinkiang in China in small numbers. They are considered one of the most religious Muslim groups of Central Asia. They are Sunnite Muslims who have kept many traditional practices including religious marriage rituals. Sunnite Muslims, who make up the majority of Muslims in the world, follow the example of the prophet Muhammad as a model for correct Muslim behaviour.

Weddings in Afghanistan

Weddings in Afghanistan are festive occasions. The wedding contract is signed in a private ceremony. Musicians welcome the bride and groom to a big gathering of family and friends. Everyone stands as the couple enters with the *Qur'an*, the Islamic holy book, held above their heads. There is singing and dancing and a large feast. Near the end of the evening, the traditional attan circle dance is performed.

Buzkashi in Afghanistan

The high plateau of Afghanistan is ideal for riding horses, and over the centuries, the people there have become highly skilled riders. They like to show these skills off, especially in a game called buzkashi, which is played at festivals, including wedding ceremonies. Buzkashi means goat killing, but today the sport is played using the body of a headless calf. Dozens of men on horseback try to pick up the calf and carry it to a scoring area. Games can last for several days, and injuries to horses and riders are quite common.

A mosque in the city of Samarkand, one of the oldest religious and cultural centres of Central Asia.

Because buzkashi is highly competitive and dangerous, both players and their horses undergo years of strict training.

The rabab, a three-stringed plucked instrument, is one of the oldest Afghan instruments. It is used to play traditional music and is found in many other Muslim countries.

The Middle East

Jewish Weddings

Marrying and raising of children form a very important part of Jewish life. Although different sects of Judaism—Orthodox, Conservative and Reform have distinct observances, they share many rituals. The wedding may be held in a synagogue (Jewish house of worship), home or even in the open air. The ceremony consists of several parts, which may or may not include the reciting of vows. After the ceremony, the guests enjoy a delicious feast and lively dancing.

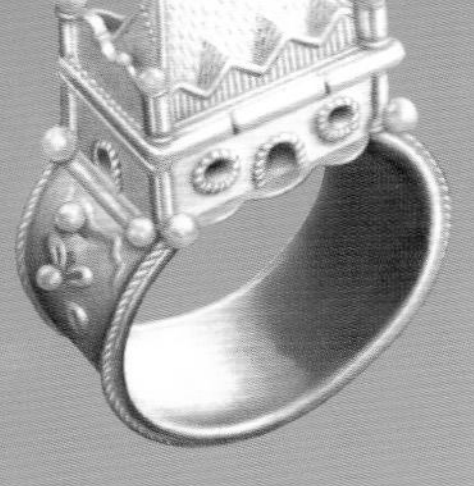

***A ring worn at a Jewish wedding** in Europe has a model of a synagogue. Such rings may also feature the newlyweds' home.*

The Mitzvot

The Mitzvot are the commandments, rules and religious duties that Jewish people believe God wants them to follow. The Mitzvot offer Jewish people guidance in every area of their life, including marriage. Some of the Mitzvot are intended to promote good relations between husband and wife.

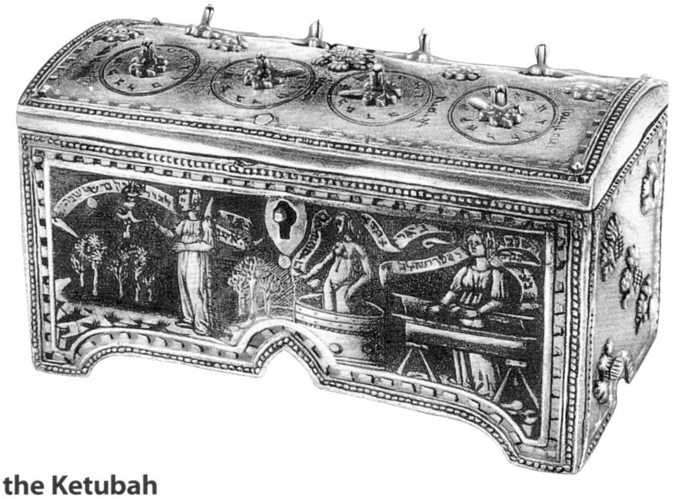

***A wedding chest shows a woman having a ritual bath** at the mikveh (special pool), to purify herself before her wedding.*

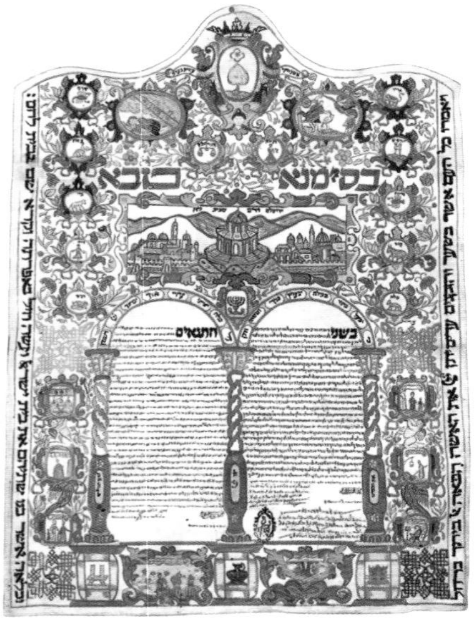

***A beautiful, ornate ketubah** is a work of art. Some married couples like to frame and display it in their home.*

Signing the Ketubah

The wedding begins with the signing of the ketubah (wedding contract). Traditionally, this document is written in the ancient language of Aramaic. Nowadays, it is often translated into the couple's language as well. The contract is a legal document in which the husband promises to feed, clothe and care for his wife. It states that if he divorces her, he will leave her money. The ketubah is read aloud. Then the groom signs the document, which is witnessed by two people. At some modern Jewish weddings, the bride signs the document, too. The ketubah belongs to the bride and is given to her for safekeeping.

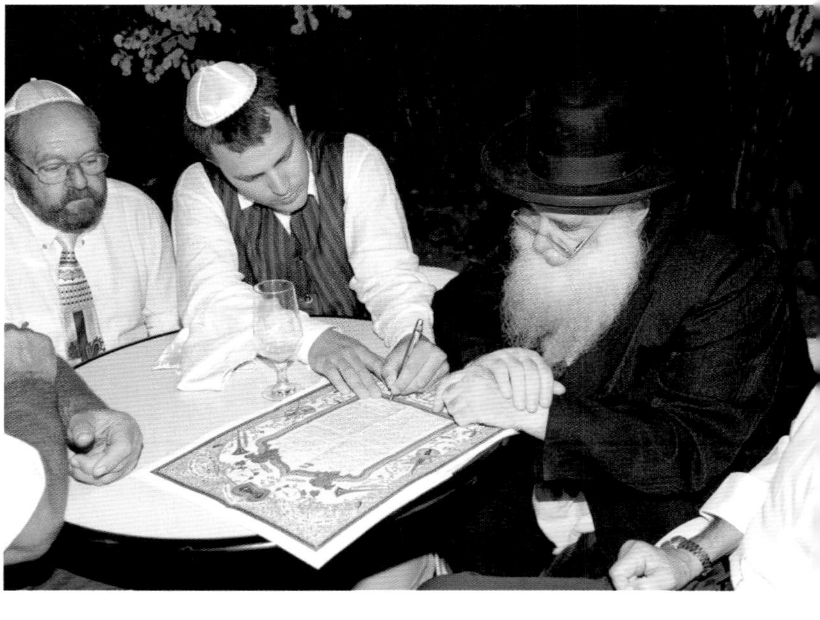

***A groom signs a ketubah** in the presence of a rabbi and two witnesses. Sometimes, a brief translation of the contract in the local language is read aloud first.*

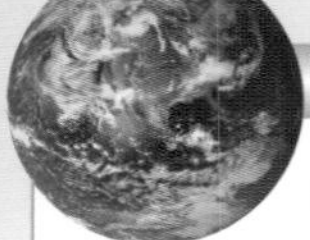

THE MIDDLE EAST

The Middle East covers parts of northern Africa, southwestern Asia and southeastern Europe. Scholars disagree on which countries make up the Middle East. But many say the region consists of Bahrain, Cyprus, Egypt, Iran, Iraq, Israel, Jordan, Kuwait, Lebanon, Oman, Qatar, Saudi Arabia, Sudan, Syria, Turkey, United Arab Emirates and Yemen. The region also is the birthplace of three major religions—Judaism, Christianity and Islam.

JACOB AND RACHEL

At some traditional weddings, a bride and groom first see each other on their wedding day at the bedeken (veiling) of the bride. The men lead the groom to a room where the bride sits with the women of her family. The groom gazes at her and then lowers a veil over her face to show that he values her for more than her beauty. The ceremony is held in memory of the Biblical story in which Jacob did not see the face of his bride Rachel before their wedding and was tricked into marrying her sister, Leah, instead.

Jacob, revered as one of the fathers of the Jewish people, meets Rachel, his future bride at a well. According to the Bible, Jacob worked for Rachel's father for 14 years to earn the right to marry her.

Under the Huppa

A Jewish wedding takes place under a huppa, a wedding canopy. The canopy is usually a cloth held up by four posts. It symbolises the shelter of God's love and the marriage and home the couple will build together. In some traditions, when the couple first enters the huppa, the bride circles the groom seven times, representing the seven wedding blessings that the rabbi will recite. The rabbi blesses a goblet of wine, and the bride and groom each take a sip. Then the two exchange rings. Then the ketubah may be read. The rabbi recites the seven blessings, which praise God and ask God to give the couple a happy life together. Finally, the bride and groom take another sip of wine.

PREPARATIONS FOR A TRADITIONAL JEWISH WEDDING may include the groom's tish which means table in Yiddish. He tries to present a lecture on the week's reading from the *Torah* while his male friends and family members heckle him. It's supposed to be fun and help the groom relax before the wedding.

Many Jewish weddings are held outdoors, a custom dating from ancient times.

Breaking the Glass

At the end of the ceremony, the groom breaks a glass under his foot. Some people believe this ritual symbolises the destruction of the ancient Jewish temple in Jerusalem. It reminds the couple that a marriage may also break if a couple does not work to keep it strong. After the glass is broken, everyone shouts "Mazel tov" (Good luck!). The couple then goes to a private room to relax for a short time before joining the celebration. If a couple has fasted all day, they will also eat something.

A LIVELY CIRCLE DANCE CALLED THE HORA is often performed by the bride, groom and guests at the reception. In another custom, the bride and groom hold on to either end of a handkerchief while sitting on chairs. Then the guests lift them high into the air.

The groom stomps on the wine glass, which is well wrapped for safety.

Muslim Traditions

The family is the basis of Islamic society. Marrying and having a family are highly recommended as activities blessed by Allah (God). As a result, Muslims consider marriage a solemn agreement, not to be undertaken lightly. They believe a marriage partner should be chosen for life. The couple meet and get to know each other before getting married, but they are not left alone together during this time. The bride and groom sign a marriage contract at the Nikah ceremony. The contract includes a gift from the groom to the bride that is called a mahr. Lavish ceremonies accompany weddings, from henna parties to elaborate feasts and entertainment.

Adam, the first man, shown with Eve, the first woman, was the first in a series of prophets to whom Allah revealed His message, according to Islamic teachings.

Ceremonies and Rituals

Muslim weddings are not considered religious ceremonies. A Muslim wedding itself is actually a civil (nonreligious) ceremony during which the bride and groom sign a contract that is also signed by two male witnesses. Joyous festivities, with banquets, live music and dancing, follow. Celebrations vary from country to country. Some may be elaborate affairs lasting up to a week. In many Islamic countries, the bride and her friends and female relatives gather for a party shortly before the wedding. During this party, the bride's hands and feet are decorated with henna (a dark reddish-brown dye). Separate parties may be held for the groom. On the last night, the bride is brought to her new home.

Musicians entertain at a wedding banquet in Agra, in northern India, in an illustration from the late 1500s.

Marriage and Islam

Although weddings are not considered religious ceremonies, the *Qur'an*, the sacred book of Islam, details the duties of a husband toward his wife and the wife's rights within marriage. The husband is responsible for looking after his wife and ensuring she has food, clothing and a comfortable home. He is to respect her and treat her with kindness. The wife receives a marriage gift—perhaps money or gold or even an education—which gives her some security for the future. A wife is instructed to be faithful and attend to the comfort of her husband. The role of women in society varies greatly throughout the Muslim world. Muslim women in some countries work outside the home, while the lives of others centre on the home and family.

A couple from Qatar watches their wedding celebration. Qatari weddings often last for several days.

A Bedouin woman in Ethiopia dances to the rhythm of men's clapping at a marriage celebration.

The Bedouin People

The name bedouin comes from the Arabic word *badawin*, meaning desert dwellers. Traditionally, Bedouins have been nomads, people who move from place to place as a way of making a living. They migrated with their herds of camels, sheep and goats. There are still Bedouin communities around the Middle East and North Africa, but is no longer common to see Bedouin in long, flowing robes riding across the desert on camels. Many Bedouin live as semi-nomads; they spend some time farming in settled communities as well as migrating with their herds. Marriages among the Rashaida Bedouin of the northeast African countries of Eritrea and Sudan are arranged within the community. Wedding celebrations may last up to a week. Young men have camel races and hold a sword-dancing competition, while young women dance. At the end, the bride leaves for the groom's home, perched on a camel.

An Egyptian bride and groom enjoy a first dance at their wedding as the bridesmaids gather around the couple.

Palestinian Traditions

In some Palestinian villages, parents traditionally arranged their children's marriages, though the bride and groom both had to agree to the arrangements. Today, Palestinian families are still strongly involved in the choice of a husband or wife. Once the families agree to the marriage, they determine the mahr (marriage gift) from the groom to the bride. At the wedding ceremony in the village square, wedding guests dance a lively dance of celebration called the dabka. The celebrations continued for anywhere between a week and a month, with much feasting.

A Bedouin money hat was traditionally worn by the Palestinian people of Hebron and other villages nearby in the mid-1800s. Such headdresses were sometimes owned by a community and lent out for brides to wear at their wedding. Money hats were decorated with many coins. Each generation added more coins until hundreds decorated a headdress.

Westernised Ceremonies

Many couples in the Middle East choose to have Western-style weddings. In Egypt, Muslim couples usually sign their marriage contract at home. Then they attend a big reception, often at a hotel or banquet hall, with a lavish meal and music. As the couple leaves the party, they may be escorted by such entertainers as belly dancers, and fire-eaters.

A Rashaida Bedouin bride wears a burqa (veil) richly embroidered with silver thread and decorated with pendants during the first year of her marriage.

Yemenite Jewish and Assyrian Christian Rituals

Over time, the customs and rituals of an ethnic or religious group may change, especially if the group is forced from its traditional homeland. Only a few hundred Jewish people remain in Yemen, a country in the southern Arabian Peninsula, where Jews first settled sometime between 200 B.C. and A.D. 200. Most of the approximately one million Assyrians live outside their ancient homeland, now northern Iraq. Fascinating reminders of these cultures appear in their wedding rituals and are examples of enduring traditions.

A chief rabbi's hat from Yemen features an ancient design.

A Yemenite Jewish bride wears a traditional headdress. Hanging around it are fresh flowers and branches of rue, believed to ward off the evil eye.

A traditional Jewish Yemenite girl's hood is called a gargush. Girls hoping to get married wore it with special decorations made of red embroidery.

The Yemenite Jewish Bride

The traditional wedding costume of a Yemenite Jewish bride differed from that of her Muslim neighbours. Her luxurious clothes included a beautiful coat dress decorated with gold thread. She wore leggings with red star motifs, a distinctively Jewish design. On her head, she wore an ornate pointed headdress embroidered with rows of pearls. Most impressive was the bride's lavish jewellery, which was crafted by Jewish silversmiths. (Traditionally, only Jews could work as silversmiths.) Decorations draped from the headdress to her chest. She wore many necklaces, made of silver and coral beads, pearls and silver bells. Her arms were covered in filigree (ornamental gold or silver) bracelets, arranged in a particular order. On her fingers, she displayed many filigree rings. Some modern Jewish Yemenites and the descendants of those who moved elsewhere still wear traditional clothing for their weddings.

A scribe writes a marriage contract.

Jewish People in Yemen

Jewish people of Yemen enjoyed relatively peaceful relations with the area's ruling Muslims from the A.D. 600s to the 1400s. In the late 1600s, however, Muslim persecution of Jewish Yemenites increased and many were forced from their home. From the late 1800s to the mid-1900s, growing opposition to a government that refused to grant them equal rights led nearly all Jewish Yemenites to migrate to what is now Israel. Few Jews remain in Yemen today.

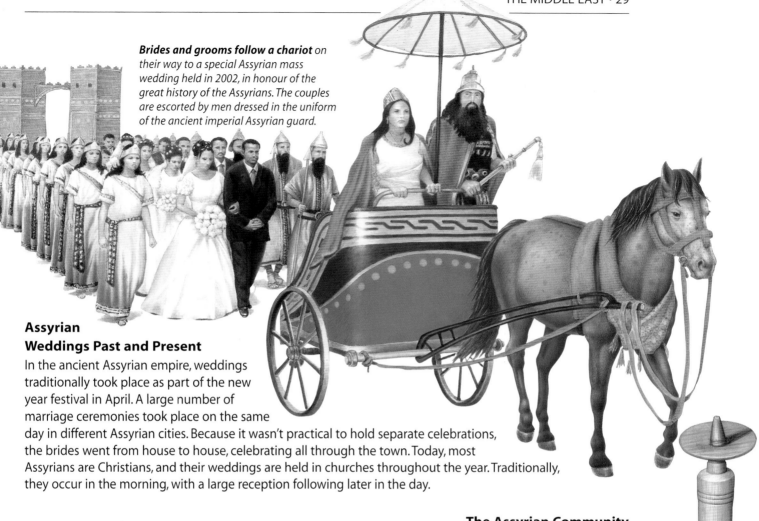

***Brides and grooms follow a chariot** on their way to a special Assyrian mass wedding held in 2002, in honour of the great history of the Assyrians. The couples are escorted by men dressed in the uniform of the ancient imperial Assyrian guard.*

Assyrian Weddings Past and Present

In the ancient Assyrian empire, weddings traditionally took place as part of the new year festival in April. A large number of marriage ceremonies took place on the same day in different Assyrian cities. Because it wasn't practical to hold separate celebrations, the brides went from house to house, celebrating all through the town. Today, most Assyrians are Christians, and their weddings are held in churches throughout the year. Traditionally, they occur in the morning, with a large reception following later in the day.

The Assyrian Community

The Assyrians are descended from the people who built the ancient Assyrian empire. The empire rose to power in Mesopotamia (now modern Iraq) more than 3,000 years ago and developed one of the highest civilisations of the ancient world. Around A.D. 1400, the Mongolian conqueror Timur destroyed many cities in the Middle East, and the Assyrian community dwindled. By the early 1900s, most Assyrians lived in what are now eastern Turkey, northern Iraq, and northern Iran. The Assyrians fought with the Allies during World War I (1914-1918), and many of them hoped to win a homeland when peace came, but they failed to achieve their dream. Since then, many Assyrians have been forced to leave their home because of persecution and seek refuge in other countries. Today, most live in Iraq, Iran, Syria and Turkey. Many also have settled in the United States.

***A married couple holding hands,** a symbol of love, is shown in this stone carving from the ancient Mesopotamian city of Babylon.*

***A zurna, a wind instrument,** is played at Assyrian weddings and other outdoor festivities.*

Western European Traditions

Some people in Western Europe marry in civil (non-religious) ceremonies. Many more marry in churches, temples or mosques, making their vows before God and a congregation of their families and friends. The details of the ceremony depend on the couple's religious group, while events before and after the ceremony vary from one country to another.

Rice was once a symbol of fertility, happiness and long life. At the end of a wedding ceremony, guests often throw rice over the newly married couple as a wish for good luck and many children.

Orange blossoms are a popular decoration for bridal headdresses in Europe.

Europe and the Americas

The exchange of rings is an important moment in a wedding.

Christian Weddings

Roman Catholics and Eastern Orthodox Christians consider marriage one of the seven sacraments through which God blesses His followers. A Roman Catholic wedding ceremony that includes celebration of a Mass may last for about an hour. There are prayers and hymns, and the bride and groom declare their vows to each other before God and the congregation of friends and relatives, and exchange rings. Protestant ceremonies also include prayers and hymns. Christians believe that marriage should be for life, even though some people get divorced.

Orange Blossoms

Orange blossoms have been used in brides' headdresses in Europe for centuries. The custom reached the United Kingdom in the early 1800s. In 1840, Great Britain's Queen Victoria (1819-1901) wore orange blossoms instead of the crown jewels at her wedding to Prince Albert (1819-1861).

Bride and groom marry in a civil wedding in France after the revolution.

EUROPE

Europe is one of the smallest of the world's seven continents in area but one of the largest in population. Europe extends from the Arctic Ocean in the north to the Mediterranean Sea in the south and from the Atlantic Ocean in the west to the Ural Mountains in the east. The 47 countries of Europe include the world's largest country, Russia, as well as the world's smallest, Vatican City. Russia lies partly in Europe and partly in Asia.

THE CIVIL MARRIAGE

In recent centuries, marriage laws and customs have changed in many societies. In France, for example, marriage laws changed dramatically during the French Revolution of 1789–1799. Before the revolution, people were required to marry in a church. After King Louis XVI (1754–1793) was overthrown and France became a republic, the revolutionaries established civil marriage, by which people marry legally without having a religious ceremony. Marriage was viewed as a contract between a man and a woman, as it was in ancient times.

Tartan Kilts at Scottish Weddings

At Scottish weddings, the groom and other men in the party sometimes wear full Highland dress. This includes a kilt (a knee-length, skirtlike garment) made of tartan (a checked cloth); a sporran (an ornamental pouch that often hangs at the front of the kilt) and a black jacket. The bride wears a white dress, over which the groom may drape a sash in his family's tartan. Before the wedding, in some parts of Scotland, a bride's friends may parade her through the town, dressed in odd clothes, while the groom's friends march him around the town carrying a creel (basket) of stones on his back until the bride rescues him with a kiss. Highland dancing to the sound of bagpipes follows the wedding.

During a champagne toast, guests raise their glasses and cheer the newlyweds.

Wedding Receptions

Although traditions vary throughout Europe, feasting and dancing often follow a wedding ceremony. Receptions may be elegant sit-down meals accompanied by an orchestra, or noisy parties where guests dance through the night. They may also last several days. In the Burgundy region of France, guests traditionally celebrated for three days by eating, drinking wine and dancing a folk dance called the Farandole. Wedding receptions serve to bring together the families of the bride and groom.

Bridegrooms and male guests of Scottish ancestry often wear traditional Highland dress, even if the wedding is not in Scotland.

CONFETTI

- 150 g almonds (shelled)
- 300 g icing sugar
- 60–125 ml water

Toast the almonds in an oven at 180°C/350° F/gas 4 until golden brown in colour. Mix the sugar and water, adding a small amount of water at a time to form a paste mixture. The mixture should be thick enough so that it can coat each almond completely. Dip the almonds individually in the mixture and place them on a sheet of greaseproof paper to dry. When the confetti are completely dry, place them in an sealed container and refrigerate.

ITALIAN BRIDES AND GROOMS present their guests with sugared almonds. These favours are known as confetti and are a symbol of the sweet and bitter things in life. Five almonds represent a wish for happiness, long life, health, wealth and fruitfulness.

THE FIRST BRIDAL SHOWER was held in the Netherlands, according to a legend about a girl who loved a miller (a person who operates a machine for grinding grain into flour). The miller was poor because of his generosity to others. But the girl's father wanted her to marry a rich man. On hearing this, the poor people the miller had helped showered the couple with gifts so they could marry.

Spanish Weddings

According to one Spanish wedding custom not found anywhere else in Europe, the groom gives the bride 13 gold coins, called arras. The coins represent his pledge that he will provide and care for her during their marriage.

Today, Spanish brides usually wear white for their wedding but traditionally their wedding gown was made of black silk.

Weddings in Eastern Europe

Many people in Eastern Europe are deeply religious. Although many people in the southern part of the region follow Islam, Christianity is eastern Europe's main religion. Countries in the western half of eastern Europe are largely Roman Catholic. Farther east, they are Eastern Orthodox. The religious part of a marriage ceremony follows a particular church's teachings, but other customs vary from one country to another. Many have their origins in folklore, superstition and old beliefs that predate Christianity. They often reflect the fact that many people lived in remote rural areas where life could be hard and people needed luck to survive.

Crowns are placed on the heads of the bride and groom at an Orthodox wedding to show that the marriage is noble and the couple will be the king and queen of their household.

Eastern Orthodox Ceremonies

The priest first blesses the rings and places them on the third finger of the bride's and groom's right hand. He then switches the rings to the other person's hand and back three times. The priest joins their right hands, prays and places a lighted candle in their left hands. Two crowns joined by a white ribbon are placed on their heads and switched back and forth three times. After the priest reads from the *Bible*, the couple takes three sips of wine from a shared cup. Then, as the choir sings three hymns, the priest leads the bride and groom three times around the wedding table on their first steps as a married couple.

An Eastern Orthodox wedding includes several rituals done three times, to represent the Father, the Son and the Holy Spirit, the three Divine Persons of the Trinity.

Jesus and His mother, Mary, attend the wedding feast at Cana in this illustration. According to the Bible, the servant filled six stone jars with water which Jesus then miraculously changed into wine.

The Wedding at Cana

Taking three sips of wine from the same cup symbolises that the couple will share everything, which will double their joys and halve their sorrows. It is a ritual performed in memory of the wedding at Cana in Galilee where, the Bible says, Jesus performed his first miracle. Jesus was invited to the wedding with his mother, Mary, and some of His disciples in the early days of His ministry. The wine ran out during the celebration. Realising that the bridegroom would be embarrassed by this, Mary told Jesus. He asked a servant to fill some large jars with water. Then, Jesus asked for some of the liquid to be taken to the chief steward. When the steward sipped it, he commented that it was the best wine he had ever tasted. Then Jesus's disciples knew that He had changed the water to wine.

CARPATHO-RUSYN WEDDING CUSTOMS

The Carpatho-Rusyns come from the area around the Carpathian Mountains in Eastern Europe and live where the borders of Slovakia, Poland and Ukraine meet. Through history, these people were conquered by many other nations and emigrated to other countries, yet many have preserved their separate identity. At one time, when a Carpatho-Rusyn woman became engaged, she gave her fiance a sprig of rosemary that he wore until the wedding. On the wedding day, her outfit included a wreath of periwinkles, symbolising everlasting affection. She waited at her parents' home for her bridegroom, who came in a procession, led by a flag bearer and followed by musicians and members of his family. When he arrived, his bride was hidden from him, and her parents tested his love by showing him various "false brides". Eventually, the real bride appeared, and the wedding party went to the church for a formal ceremony conducted according to the ancient Byzantine Rite. After the ceremony, celebrations began with dancing and singing, which usually lasted for days. Today, the celebration lasts only one day and is often held in a restaurant.

A traditional wedding is reenacted in the museum of Carpatho-Rusyn culture in Svidnik, in northeastern Slovakia. The performance of these rituals are one of the ways this culture is kept alive.

Bridesmaids

A Polish bride usually has several bridesmaids. During the reception, they and other women surround the bride for the "unveiling" ritual. An unmarried woman, usually the maid of honour, removes the bride's crown of leaves and flowers and her veil after the wedding. Then a married woman replaces them with a special cap traditionally worn by married women. This ritual represents the bride's entry into the world of married women.

Bread and Salt

In many Eastern European countries, wedding guests are traditionally greeted with a small gift of bread and salt. In Poland, the parents of the bride and groom present bread sprinkled with salt and a goblet of wine to the newly married couple at the reception. The bread is a wish that the couple never goes hungry. The salt reminds them that life may be hard at times, and the wine is to wish them good health, good fortune and many good friends.

Salted bread and a warm welcome from their parents greet a bride and groom in Poland.

A bride's friends in a Polish village weave her wedding crown from flowers, ribbons and the leaves of rosemary and other herbs.

IN THE CZECH REPUBLIC, legend says that a bride will live as long as the tree planted in her garden by her friends. The tree is decorated with coloured ribbons and painted eggshells. In contrast, Greeks break plates on the floor at the reception for good luck and then dance on the pieces.

The Americas: Before the Wedding

A diamond traditionally adorns an engagement ring, though emeralds, sapphires and rubies are also popular gems for engagement rings.

Some of the customs surrounding courtship and wedding planning are shared by people in Europe and the Americas. Many individuals find a marriage partner during a period of dating and courtship. Traditionally, the man proposes—that is, asks the woman to marry him. Once the couple has decided to marry and has chosen a wedding date, they prepare for the big day. During this time, friends and family often help the bride and groom plan the wedding and reception.

Gifts from family and friends help newlyweds begin their life together. Many couples register at local stores, listing household items they need or would like to own.

FOR THE AMISH PEOPLE marriage and the family are very important. At about age 16, boys and girls may begin attending social activities separately from their parents, looking for a suitable partner. But most Amish don't marry until about age 20. During these years, young people also make a commitment to live according to Amish ways and formally join the church by being baptised. Both the bride and groom must be baptised Amish church members to be married in an Amish ceremony.

The Proposal

In the past, a man who wanted to marry a woman first asked her father's permission. Today, however, he normally asks the woman directly, after going out with her for a while. Sometimes, a woman will propose to a man. After a couple becomes engaged, the man usually buys the woman a ring to wear on the third finger of her left hand. In Brazil, for example, when man proposes to a woman, he may give her an odd number of roses and tell her that she is the missing rose in the bunch. Brazilian suitors also give their women a wedding band to be worn on the right hand until the wedding ceremony, during which it is then placed on the left hand. During the engagement, which can last from a few days to several years, plans are made for the wedding and the couple's new life together.

THE AMERICAS

The continents of North America and South America make up the Western Hemisphere. North America contains Canada, Greenland, the United States, Mexico, Central America and the Caribbean Sea islands. South America contains Argentina, Bolivia, Brazil (which occupies almost half the continent), Chile, Colombia, Ecuador, Guyana, Paraguay, Peru, Suriname, Uruguay and Venezuela.

A U.S. Marine corporal kneels to propose to the woman he wishes to marry in a traditional gesture.

Wedding Preparations

In addition to sending wedding invitations to family and friends, many couples publicly announce their engagement or wedding date in local newspapers. The period before the wedding is an exciting time for both the groom and bride. The bride is often given a bridal shower, where guests bring gifts for the engaged couple. Popular gifts are kitchen appliances, dinnerware and other home furnishings. Sometime before the wedding, both bride and groom may go out, separately, with friends for a night of fun to relieve pre-wedding tension.

A bridal bouquet traditionally is made of white flowers, though many modern brides choose brightly coloured flowers. The bride carries the bouquet at the wedding ceremony.

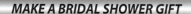

MAKE A BRIDAL SHOWER GIFT

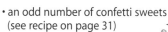

- an odd number of confetti sweets (see recipe on page 31)
- a wooden spoon
- a piece of fabric
- ribbon
- a note card
- a hole punch
- a coloured pen or marker

Place an odd number (three or five is considered lucky) of confetti sweets in the spoon and cover the spoon and confetti with the fabric. Tie a ribbon around the fabric to secure the confetti in place. Punch a hole in the note card. Write good wishes for the bride and groom and then tie the card to the ribbon.

A dressmaker puts the finishing touches on a bridal gown. Picking the right wedding dress is an important activity for the bride.

GAY UNIONS

Until almost the end of the 1900s, legal marriages were limited to those between a man and a woman. Although many lesbians and gay men lived in long-term relationships, they could not claim the same marital rights as heterosexual couples. After much campaigning by lesbians and gays, the situation slowly began to change in some countries. In 2001, the Netherlands became the first country to recognise same-sex marriages and give those who entered them the same legal status and rights as married heterosexual couples. Some other countries, including Denmark, France, Germany, Iceland, Norway and Sweden, give same-sex partners some, but not all, such legal rights.

Gay couples parade down the streets of Washington D.C. during a gay rights march.

Weddings in the Americas

Marriage customs and traditions vary throughout the Americas because of the great variety of ethnic groups that live there. The oldest customs are those of Native Americans, though many of these ways were lost as settlers from Europe took their land and banned their traditions. European settlers brought new religious and cultural traditions with them to the United States and Canada. Many common American marriage ceremonies and rituals do not have a religious origin. Some, such as carrying the bride over the threshold, have their origins in ancient tradition. Others, such as weddings in Las Vegas, Nevada, conducted by a person dressed as singer Elvis Presley, reflect modern culture. Many people choose a civil ceremony conducted by a judge or other government official rather than a religious one.

Jumping over a broom sometimes symbolised marriage between African American slaves, who were not allowed to marry officially.

TRADITIONALLY MANY ALGONQUIAN-SPEAKING PEOPLE MARRIED OUTDOORS and made their vows to the Creator (God) before a tribal official known as the Pipe Carrier. When the Pipe Carrier was convinced that they were serious about their commitment to each other, the couple declared that they wanted to be husband and wife. They then smoked from the Pipe Carrier's pipe.

"SOMETHING OLD, SOMETHING NEW, SOMETHING BORROWED, SOMETHING BLUE, AND A SILVER SIX PENCE IN YOUR SHOE" is a rhyme from the Victorian period (1837-1901) describing what a bride should wear for good luck on her wedding day.

A fringed white sash traditionally was a part of a Hopi bride's wedding clothing. The groom's male relatives made the braided sash for her.

An exchange of valuable gifts between the families of the bride and groom is an important part of Hopi marriage.

People of the Southwest

Among the Hopi, in what is now the southwestern United States, a bride traditionally stayed with her future mother-in-law before the wedding. There, she cooked and ground corn. Meanwhile, the groom and his male relatives spun cotton thread and wove the bride's wedding clothing. After the couple was married, they moved to their new home, which was usually near the bride's mother. Today, some Hopi couples choose aspects of the traditional marriage customs to include in their own wedding celebrations.

A newly married couple lock their fingers together to hold the knife used to cut the first piece of wedding cake at their reception.

Celebrations in North America

The people of North America come from many different religious and cultural backgrounds, which are reflected in varying marriage ceremonies. Once the formalities are completed, however, some customs are now common to nearly all wedding celebrations. The guests are usually invited to a meal either at the bride's parents' home or at a restaurant or hotel. After this meal, the bride and groom cut the cake and feed each other the first slice. The groom then removes the bride's garter from her leg and throws it to the unmarried male guests. The bride throws her bouquet to the unmarried female guests. According to tradition, the people who catch these items will be the next to marry (but not necessarily each other).

Las Vegas Wedding

Las Vegas, Nevada, is the wedding capital of the world, with at least 100,000 weddings taking place there each year. Some couples choose a traditional ceremony in a hotel or wedding chapel, but there are plenty of unusual settings, including hot-air balloons and helicopters as well as drive-through chapels. Settings for themed weddings include Camelot (with decorations linked to the legend of Britain's King Arthur) and ancient Egypt.

A super-stretch limo for transit from a hotel to a wedding chapel is often part of the arrangements for a Las Vegas wedding.

IN THE UNITED STATES, WEDDINGS ARE SOMETIMES CONDUCTED OUTDOORS, for example, in the garden of the bride's family home or at the seashore. The couple may make their vows before a minister, priest, rabbi or judge while standing under a specially constructed arch of roses or other sweet-smelling flowers.

Ceremonies in Cuba

The Cuban government recognises only those marriages conducted by government lawyers in special government offices, such as the Palacio de los Matrimonios in Havana. However, after this official ceremony, some couples have their wedding vows blessed in an unofficial ceremony conducted by a priest in one of the Roman Catholic churches on the island.

Although they are required to marry in a government office, Cuban brides often wear a long white dress and a veil and are attended by bridesmaids.

Carrying the bride over the threshold may reflect an ancient ritual to protect the bride during the change from single to married life.

Over the Threshold

The custom of carrying the bride over the threshold of her new home began with the ancient Romans, though no one really knows why. Some people think the Romans believed it would be a terrible sign and bad luck if the bride tripped while crossing the threshold of her new home.

Wedding guests often decorate the bridal couple's car with signs so that everyone knows that they are newlyweds.

Driving Away Together

After the solemnity of the wedding ceremony, many guests like to have some fun with the newlyweds during their first night as a married couple. In a French tradition known as shivaree (spelled charivari in French), a crowd clanged pots and pans, rang bells and fired shotguns to disturb the couple, who then had to appear in their wedding clothes and provide their tormentors with treats. Present-day fun includes tying tin cans to the bumper of the honeymoon car to make noise.

JUST MARRIED
MARY
AND
SAM
CONGRATULATIONS
13336X

West and North African Rites

Northern Africa stretches from the Atlantic Ocean in the west to the Red Sea in the east. It runs from the busy, breezy Mediterranean Sea in the north to the hot, barren Sahara in the south. The various ethnic groups and cultures within this vast area prepare for and celebrate weddings in different ways. Many communities follow the wedding traditions of Islam, northern Africa's major religion, but they also include more ancient customs. Brides often wear a veil for some days before the wedding. Women perform dances separately from men. Some wedding ceremonies last a day; others, a week. Married couples generally live with the husband's family. But in some cultures, they set up a household with the wife's family.

This traditional Moroccan Berber bride's crown is made of coral, leather and monkey fur, with hanging silver pendants.

In Nigeria, the groom's family gives the bride a wedding basket containing engraved calabashes. Calabashes are made from dried gourds which are embellished and displayed in the home.

A Gift for the Bride

In some parts of northern Africa, the bride's and groom's families agree to a wedding contract. The groom's family gives gifts to the bride's family, usually money, jewellery and animals such as cattle and camels. The bride takes these gifts, called the bride price, to her new home. Bororo nomad women of northwestern Africa receive dozens of calabashes as part of their bride price. These decorated, hollowed-out gourds are tied to a special pack animal and carried from camp to camp. They are the most valuable possession a Bororo wife has and are displayed only at special ceremonies.

Attracting Women

The men of the Bororo tribe in northern Niger, a country in western Africa, try to attract a bride by making exaggerated facial expressions during a dance called the yaake (dance of charm). The dance takes place during a festival held at the end of the dry season. The Bororo, whose men are cattle herders, hold the festival to celebrate the arrival of the annual rains and the hope of new green pastures. Young Bororo herders dance the yaake in front of young Bororo women. They try to charm the women by grinning from ear to ear, blowing their cheeks out and boggling their eyes.

Young Bororo men perform the yaake wearing makeup and their finest embroidered and beaded clothes. Their headdresses are decorated with ostrich plumes.

AFRICA

Africa lies south of Europe and west of Asia and contains 53 independent countries. Tropical rain forests dominate western and central Africa. The world's largest desert, the Sahara, stretches across northern Africa. Africa also has the world's longest river—the Nile. Much of the continent is grassland. In the north, most of the people are Arabs. The great majority of the African population lives south of the Sahara.

Africa

Paying the Price

The nomadic Tuareg breed and herd camels, goats, cattle and sheep across much of northwestern Africa. In Tuareg society, young men and women get to know each other at a large gathering called a Tendi. The women sit in a circle and sing love songs, while the men try to attract their attention by prancing around on their camels. Weddings are publicly announced by blacksmiths, people thought to have spiritual powers. At the wedding, the bride is hidden at first in a tent attended by her female friends and relatives. A procession brings her to the groom, and they are joined in marriage. A special hut is built for the couple to live in at the bride's family camp.

A Tuareg wedding party makes its way to the ceremony. Even the donkeys are decorated with fine cloths and coloured, patterned leather cushions.

Berber Brides

In Morocco, Berber Women of the Atlas Mountains hold a "henna night" on the eve of a wedding. This is a party for the bride, her friends and female family members. At the party, the bride's body is painted with delicate patterns using henna, a paste made from the powdered leaves of the henna plant. After the henna dries on the skin and falls off, a coloured stain ranging from orange to black remains. Although all the other women are decorated on "henna night", the bride gets the most attention. The older women also use this night to explain to the bride her duties as a wife, but there is a lot of fun, too!

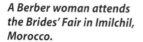

A Berber woman attends the Brides' Fair in Imilchil, Morocco.

A Berber woman at the Brides' Fair in Imilcil, Morocco.

A Berber woman performs the guedra dance of love on her knees, below. The dance is said to have a hypnotic effect on men.

The Brides' Fair

Some Moroccan Berbers living in the Atlas Mountains are allowed to choose their own marriage partners. This custom is linked to a legend about a young woman named Tislet and a young man named Isli who wanted to marry. But their families were enemies. So after promising to love each other forever, they committed suicide. The tears shed for them created Isli and Tislet, two lakes separated by a mountain. For hundreds of years, Berbers have travelled to the yearly lakeside Imilchil Brides' Fair to choose a partner. At the fair, young women who have never married wear a rounded cap. Divorced or widowed women wear a peaked cap.

Customs South of the Sahara

Southern Africa stretches from dry grasslands in the north to the coastal lowlands in the south. In many societies throughout this region, a groom gives a bride price for his wife-to-be. In return, the bride performs a ceremony to show that she will work hard for him. Before the wedding, the bride is pampered with beauty treatments. A wedding headdress or heavy necklace shows her new status. Dancing is often part of the ceremony.

Husband and wife figures are carved into a stool. The stool was made from a single piece of wood by a Luba sculptor from Congo (Kinshasa) in central Africa.

Himba Brides

In the Himba herding communities of Namibia in southwest Africa, parents usually choose partners for their children. When daughters marry, they move from their parents' home to live with their husband's family. Before leaving, a bride receives special attention from her mother. The mother moisturises and perfumes her daughter's body with ochre (a type of earth used as a pigment), butterfat and sweet-smelling herbs. In addition to presenting her daughter with jewellery made of iron beads, a mother gives her an ekori (ceremonial headdress) that is passed down from generation to generation.

Accepting the Couple

Zulu bridesmaids of South Africa prepare the bride by dressing her as an adult woman for the first time. A new pleated leather skirt shows that she is to be married. The wedding ceremony includes a series of powerful warrior dances performed by the young men. At the end of the ceremony, the bride's mother-in-law smears the bride with animal fat to show that she is accepted into the family.

A young Himba woman dances for a bride, her best friend before a wedding. Other women perform ondjongo, a courting dance that mimics herders and their cattle.

A young Zulu woman wears a beaded headdress, to show she is married. The designs represent her ancestry.

Umhlanga dancers wear beaded aprons. The colours show different stages of a young woman's life. Woollen sashes and tassels are draped from the apron and around the neck. Seed pods around the ankles rattle in time to the dance.

A Royal Reed Dance

The fantastic celebration of Umhlanga takes place each year in Swaziland. Umhlanga is a royal reed dance performed partly to honour the Swazi queen mother. The dance tells the Swazi story of creation. In this story, the first human beings emerged from a single reed that was split in half along its length. The ceremony also takes place to celebrate Swazi girls' passage to womanhood. In addition, it is traditionally the time when the king chooses his new wives. Umhlanga takes place over seven days. First, thousands of young Swazi women walk to the river and collect reeds. Then they bring them back to Lobamba, the royal capital. There the reeds are woven into fences that are used to surround the queen mother's palace. On the sixth day, the women perform a rhythmic march before the queen mother and the king.

Hands and Feet

Swahili women from the east coast of Africa spend several days preparing a bride for her wedding. First, coconut oil and perfume are massaged over the bride's body. Then, the bride's hands and arms, legs and feet are decorated with fine designs. The designs are painted on with a stick that has been dipped into a paste made of henna leaf and lime juice. The bride sends the groom a present of cosmetics, too. Before the ceremony, the groom visits his veiled bride and gives her a gold or coral necklace, and her attendants dance and sing. The wedding ceremony itself is conducted by men.

Striking black designs are created with layers of henna paste. The paste is left on the skin for several hours before it is removed. Lime juice darkens the designs.

Masai boys and young men gather together at a wedding. They perform dances in front of each other to show their strength and agility.

A Fresh Life for the New Wife

Masai cattle herders live on the vast grasslands of eastern Africa. After a Masai wedding, the bride's father blesses her by spitting a mouthful of milk under her necklaces. Then he sends her to her husband's homestead, warning her not to look back at her home or she will turn to stone. The groom's best man sets off first to make sure that there are no dangers along the way. When the bride reaches her new home, the women there throw cow dung at her and shout out rudely. This ceremony warns the new bride that life as a wife can be difficult. A Masai man usually has several wives, a situation that sometimes causes problems for a new bride. The other wives may also give her a lot of support.

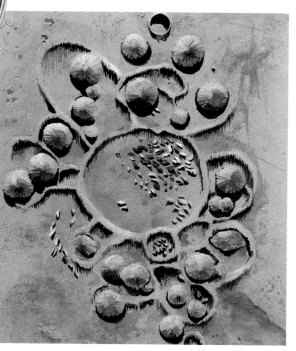

Masai women use only certain colours to make their necklaces. This wedding necklace uses mainly basic Masai colours, which are blue, orange, green, red and white.

Masai Family Households

Each wife of a Masai man must build her own hut. A Masai hut is made of branches and grass held together with a mixture of cow dung, clay and water. The huts lie close together but are fenced in so that the wives have their privacy. The first and second wife's huts lie on either side of the gate that leads to the husband's enkang (circular compound). At night, the Masai's precious cattle are herded into the enkang, which is surrounded by all the huts for protection.

This bird's-eye view of a Masai village shows cattle in the enkang, the circular compound surrounded by huts.

Marriage in the Pacific

European settlers brought Christianity to Australia and New Zealand in the 1800s. Most people there are now Christian and marry according to Christian rites, following traditional western practices. Native people, such as the Aborigines, may still follow their own customs. Among the diverse peoples and cultures of Oceania, weddings tend to embrace age-old traditions native to these Pacific Islands. Tradition there governs not only rituals but also the roles men and women play in society.

This stone axe decorated with feathers is typical of the axes given by grooms in Irian Jaya in Indonesia as part of a bride's price to the bride's family.

Australasia and Oceania

Marrying Outside the Totem

Each Aborigine tribe in Australia has its own totem, a protective mythological spirit thought to connect the people of the tribe with their ancestors. The totem, which takes the form of an animal or plant, directs a tribe's organisation, customs and ceremonies. Aborigine society requires a man to choose his wife from a different totem group. Traditionally, Aborigines did not hold formal wedding ceremonies. Some tribes staged a make-believe battle in which the groom had to shield himself from spears thrown at him by the bride's brothers. In Aboriginal weddings today, a fire stick is sometimes placed between the couple. Lighting the stick marks the moment of marriage.

A bark painting shows animals, such as the eagle, dingo and wallaby, used as totems by different clans.

Weddings on the Beach

Wedding ceremonies held on a beach are becoming increasingly popular all over the Pacific. Many couples from different parts of the world choose to marry in warm climates or faraway locations to extend their wedding celebration into a holiday, away from the routine of everyday life. Breathtaking natural landscapes, like those found in the Pacific, attract couples who wish to make their wedding day an unforgettable experience.

Newlyweds pose in the warm sun on a beach in Melbourne, along Australia's southeastern coast.

AUSTRALASIA AND OCEANIA

Australasia and Oceania lie east of Asia and west of the Americas. Australasia refers to Australia, New Guinea, New Zealand and other nearby islands. New Guinea and New Zealand are also considered as part of the Pacific Islands, or Oceania. Oceania is a name given to a group of many thousands of islands scattered across the Pacific Ocean. New Guinea is the largest island in the group. It contains Irian Jaya, which is a part of Indonesia, and the independent country of Papua New Guinea. Islands near the mainland of Asia (Indonesia, Japan, the Philippines) are part of Asia. Islands near North and South America (the Aleutians, the Galapagos) are grouped with those continents. Australia is itself a continent.

BARK CLOTH

Barkcloth is a type of cloth made from the inner bark of trees. It is made in most parts of Oceania, where it is commonly referred to as tapa. Each region has its own special technique for making tapa, though the basic process is the same. The smooth, threadlike inner bark of mulberry trees is stripped off, soaked in water and beaten. This process is repeated many times until the material is thin and soft. In many regions, the cloth is coloured and decorated with designs, then used to make clothing, blankets and wallhangings. Barkcloth is also used in Hawaii, Fiji, Tahiti, Tonga and Samoa as ground coverings for wedding ceremonies and as burial cloth for high-ranking chiefs.

A Samoan bride wears a siapo (barkcloth) dress coloured with dyes made from clay found in the Samoan mountains.

A Fijian couple sits surrounded by barkcloth wallhangings and floor mats. The bride and groom are wearing garments made especially for them on their wedding day.

Weddings in Fiji

Wedding preparations in Fiji take a lot of hard work. Just a few hours before the wedding, barkcloth, known there as masi, is made especially for the occasion for both the bride and groom to wear. Garlands made of fresh flowers called leis are also made to be worn around the neck. For the celebration, the traditional feast called lovo is prepared. Men dig pits into the ground to make lovos (underground ovens). Heated rocks are placed at the bottom of the pit and then food wrapped in coconut and banana leaves is placed on top. The pit is then covered with dirt or sand, and the buried food is left to cook for a few hours.

Bridal Currency

For many Oceanic cultures, marriage is not only the union of two people but also a contract or agreement between two clans or tribes. These contracts often involve an exchange of currency (money) or material goods. On the Santa Cruz Islands, part of the Solomon Islands, the bride price may be very high. In the past, special currency made from bird feathers was prepared especially for the occasion. This process, carried out by three men, lasted several months and involved rituals and magic.

Family Life in Papua New Guinea

Young men of the Trobriand Islands in Papua New Guinea leave the family household when they reach puberty. They live with other village men of the same age. After a young man marries, he and his wife normally live with the wife's brother. The marriage must be approved by the parents of both the bride and groom. Many gifts are exchanged between the families before the marriage.

A brother heads his unmarried sister's household in the Trobriand Islands. Once he is married, he is required to share the year's harvest with her family.

More than 50,000 feathers make up this example of bridal currency. Shells functioned as magical objects called amulets.

Glossary

Altar A table or raised platform on which offerings are placed, usually found in a church, temple or other place of worship.

Ancestor A family member from a preceding generation to whom you are directly related, for example, a grandfather or great-grandfather.

Astrologer A person who claims to know and interpret the supposed influence of the stars and planets on people or future events.

Auspicious Bringing good luck.

Banquet A feast or formal dinner held on a special occasion and usually for many people.

Betrothed Promised in marriage.

Blessing Divine favour or protection. An approval or wish for happiness.

Bride price A gift or payment made by a prospective husband or his family to the family of the bride.

Caste One of the social classes into which Hindus are divided.

Ceremony The celebration of an important event with an act or series of acts that follow a set of instructions established by a religion, culture or country.

Charm To please, delight or attract someone. Any object worn or carried by a person, or a word or act, intended to bring luck or avoid evil.

Compatible Able to get along with someone.

Courtship The time when a couple gets to know each other before getting married.

Culture A way of life. Every human society has a culture that includes its arts, beliefs, customs, institutions, inventions, language, technology and values.

Divorce The legal ending of a marriage.

Dowry Money or property given by a woman or her family to her husband when she marries him.

Engagement A promise to marry.

Faithfulness A state of being true or trustworthy and keeping a promise.

Fertility The ability to produce and reproduce living things. Land is fertile when many crops can grow there.

Fortune Happiness or good luck that happens in a person's life.

Fortune-telling Telling or claiming to tell what will happen in the future.

Friar A man who belongs to a religious order.

Go-between A person who carries messages and arranges meetings between other people.

Guru In Sikhism, one of ten early leaders of religious faith. In Hinduism, a spiritual teacher.

Henna A dark reddish-brown dye made from the leaves of a tree that grows in the tropical areas of Asia and Africa.

Horsemanship The art of riding horses.

Magistrate A government official or judge who is able to apply the law.

Matchmaker A person who arranges or tries to arrange marriages for others.

Minority A group of people with their own identity who are outnumbered by larger groups.

Mosque A place of worship and prayer for the followers of Islam.

Muslim A person who follows the religion of Islam.

Nomad A person who moves from place to place to find food for himself or herself or his or her livestock.

Officiant A person who performs or leads a ceremony, such as a priest or judge.

Pamper To treat and indulge someone with great care, attention and love.

Persecution The punishment and harassment of a person or a group of people because of their beliefs and principles, such as their religion, or because of their race or gender, or other personal characteristics.

Procession A parade held for a religious ceremony or ritual.

Prophet A person who has been inspired by God and communicates God's will or interprets God's message to the people.

Proposal An offer, which may be an offer of marriage.

Prosperous Successful; thriving; doing well; fortunate.

Puberty The stage during which a child physically develops into an adult.

Reception A social gathering to receive and welcome people that may follow a ceremony or formal occasion.

Recite To say something, such as a prayer or verse, to an audience or in a group of people.

Ritual A set of repeated actions done in a precise way, usually with a solemn meaning or significance.

Sacrament A ceremony or practice that is an outward sign that a faithful worshipper is receiving God's blessing.

Sacred Holy or precious.

Sect A group of people who share the same beliefs, principles or opinions.

Sermon A public religious speech made by a priest or minister.

Solemn Serious; done with ceremony; connected with religion; sacred.

Soothsayer A person who claims to tell what will happen in the future.

Spirit A good or bad supernatural being or force.

Suitor A man who is courting a particular woman whom he would like to marry.

Superstition A belief or practice that is the result of an unreasonable fear. The belief that magic affects events.

Symbolise To stand for or represent.

Synagogue A Jewish house of worship and a centre of Jewish education and social life.

Torah The Hebrew name for the first five books of the *Bible*.

Tradition The beliefs, opinions, customs and stories passed from generation to generation by word of mouth or by practice.

Vow A solemn promise made to another person or to God.

Ward off To keep something away.

Widow A woman whose husband is dead and who has not married again. A widower is a man whose wife is dead and who has not married again.

Index